I0177720

Stephen Hogue

I PROMISE

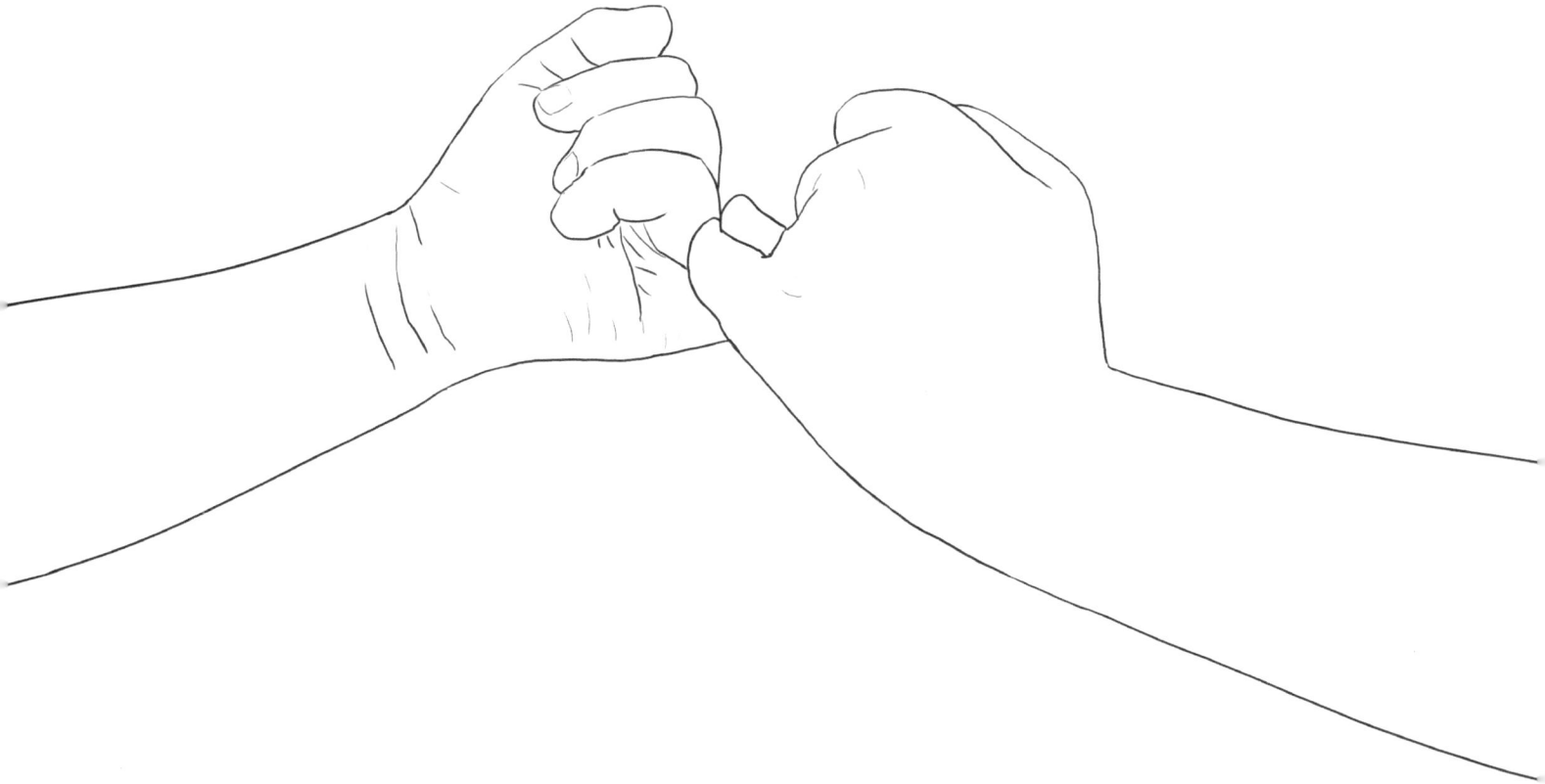

illustrated by: Kai Kanhai

Illustrated by: Kai Kanhai

DEDICATION

I dedicate this book to the almost half a million kids in the US Foster Care system. God knows them, He sees them and He loves them.

I want to thank Jennie Bishop for her collaboration, insight, and wisdom regarding this book.

"Are you coming to my baseball game today, Dad?"
Justin asked.
"I'll be there, buddy!" his dad said. **"I promise!"**

Justin watched for his dad's red truck. But his dad didn't come. He didn't keep his **promise**.

Justin's mom **promised** she would call every week.

But she didn't. She didn't keep her **promise**.

Justin's dad **promised** to play catch or go to the beach. But usually it didn't happen. He didn't always keep his **promises.**

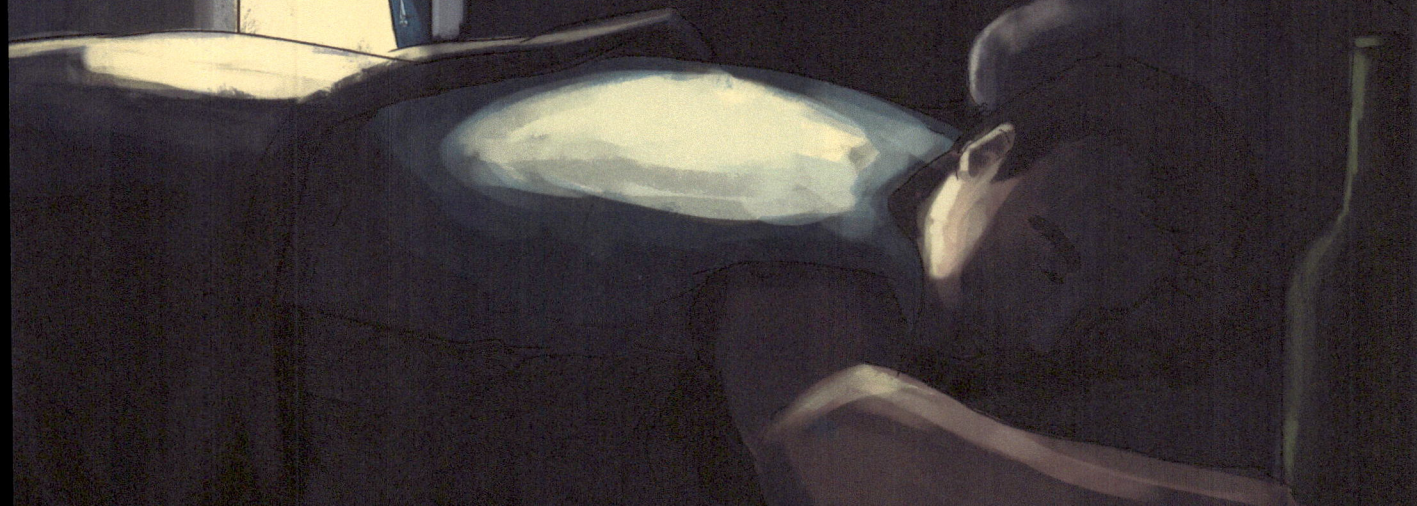

Sometimes Dad forgot to buy food.
Then Justin went to bed hungry.

GRRRRRRR

Dad **promised** to pick Justin up after school, but he didn't.
Justin was left alone. His dad hadn't kept his **promise** again.

A kind lady came to Justin's side. "I am going to make sure someone takes care of you," she said. "You will be safe. I **promise**." Justin was afraid and upset. He didn't believe her. No one kept their **promises**.

Justin and the lady drove to a big house. "This is a foster home, Justin," said the lady. "A kind family has invited you to stay for a while until your dad can get better. They will take care of you, make meals for you, take you to school and help with whatever you need."

A smiling family was at the door. The little girl said, "Hi! I'm Sophia. We have bikes and skateboards and all kinds of things to play with. You'll have a good time here, I **promise**!" But Justin didn't believe her.

This strange home was scary for Justin. The family was nice to him, but he missed his own home and bed. He missed his dad.

"You can have my teddy bear," said Sophia. "He will help you feel better. I **promise**."

The teddy bear did make Justin feel better.
Soon he was asleep.

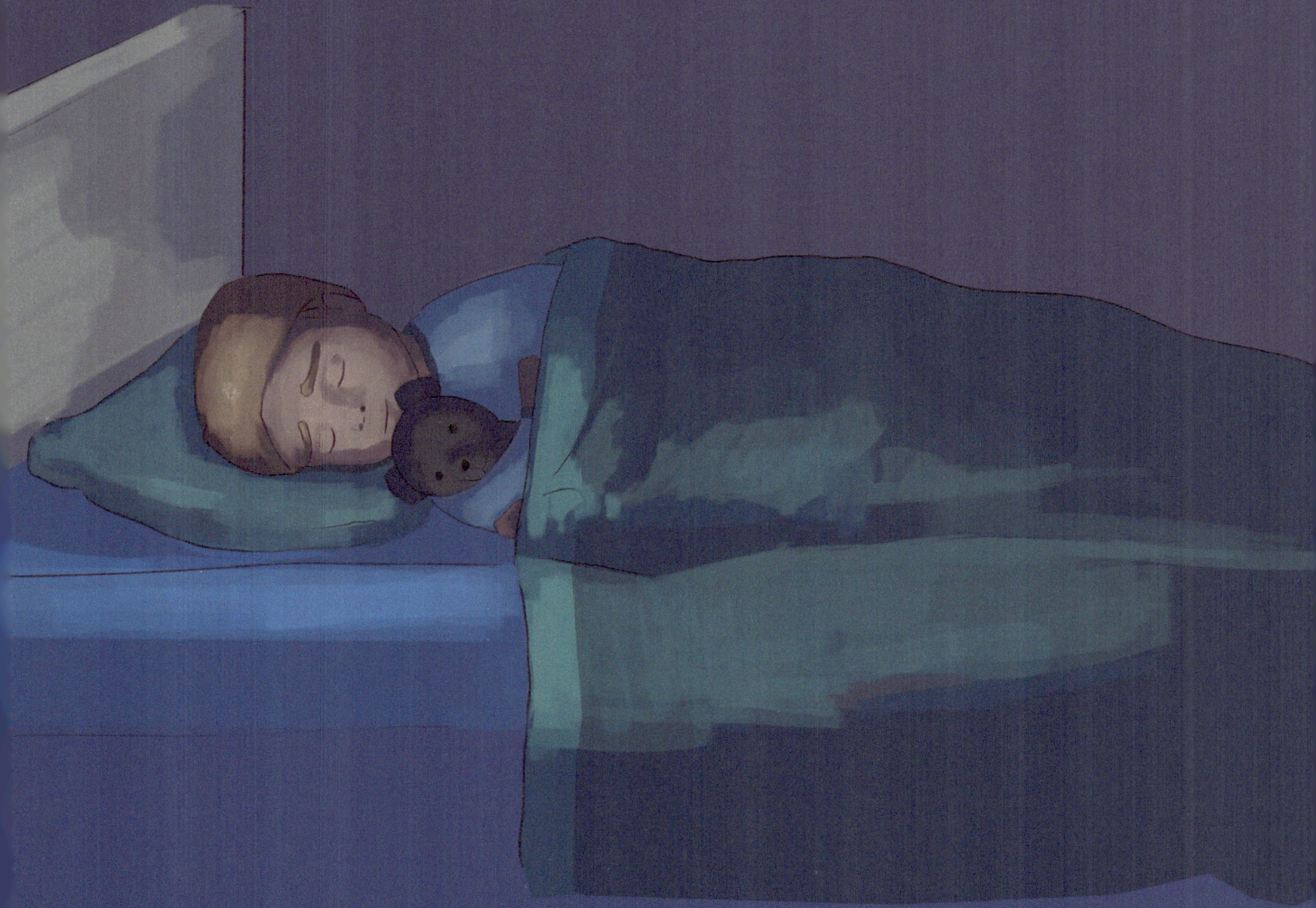

The next morning, Mrs. Franklin made Justin a good hot breakfast with fluffy eggs and buttered toast and orange juice. He was used to cereal without milk or fast food or nothing at all.

After breakfast, the Franklins took Justin and the other children to school.

"We **promise** to be here to pick you up at the end of the day," Mr. Franklin said.

And they did.

On Sunday the Franklin family took Justin to church. Justin had never gone to a church service before. He liked the beautiful windows and the choir singing.

The pastor said, "God never breaks His **promises**." Justin's ears perked up.

"God is perfect," said the pastor. "He will never leave us. He forgives us when we make mistakes. He will never stop loving us."

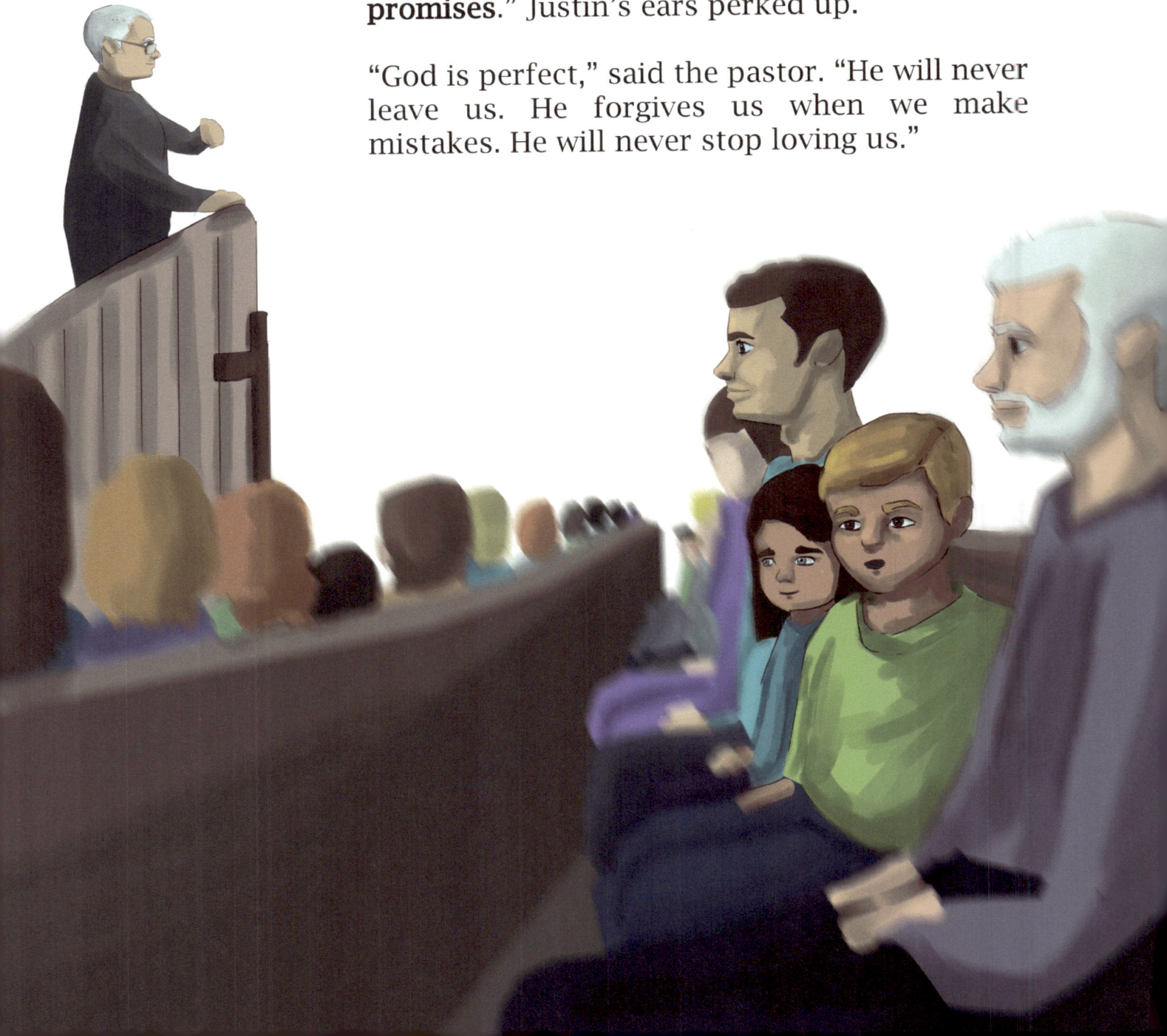

"I want to know about God,"
Justin whispered to Sophia.

That night, Justin learned more about God and His **promises**.

"We will pray for you always, Justin," the Franklins said. "We **promise**."

And they did.

Justin grew up and one day he got
a job. He **promised** to be on time.
And he was.

Justin **promised** to be faithful to God.
And he was.

A sweet young woman became Justin's friend. Justin **promised** to be her husband and the father of their children. And he was.

Justin learned to keep his **promises**.

One day Justin visited his father. The old man was sad and sorry for not keeping his **promises**.

"That's okay, Dad," said Justin. "I forgive you. And Jesus **promises** to forgive you, too."

And Justin and Jesus did!

God's Promises to Us

"I promise never to break My promises."
"No, I will not break my covenant; I will not take back one word of what I said."
2 Corinthians 1:19-20 TLB

"I promise I will never leave you."
God has said, "I will never leave you. I will never desert you." *Hebrews 13:5 NIrV*

"I promise to comfort you when you're sad."
The Lord will comfort his people. He will show his tender love to those who are suffering. *Isaiah 49:13 NIV*

"I promise to help you be calm and peaceful."
"You will keep in perfect peace him whose mind is steadfast, because he trusts in You. *Isaiah 26:3 NIV*

"I promise to keep you safe."
"Then no harm will befall you, no disaster will come near your tent". *Psalm 91:10 NIV*

"I promise to forgive your sins."
"If we confess our sins, he will forgive our sins." *1 John 1:9 NIrV*

"I promise that I will never stop loving you."
"Give thanks to the Lord, because he is good. His faithful love continues forever." *Psalm 136:1 NIrV*

Remember, even when others break their **promises,**
God never will!

What You Can Do for Children Like Justin

In America, there are almost half a million kids like Justin. To give you a mental picture, **that's 35 football fields** filled with kids standing side by side! These kids have been hurt by abuse or neglect and sometimes left alone. The United States Foster Care system was made to help them. It includes traditional family homes, but there aren't enough, so thousands live in group homes, which are like modern day orphanages.

Like Justin, children can live with a foster family or in a group home with other children until their parents get the help they need.

You can **talk to God** about kids like Justin. You can ask God to help kids who are in Foster Care. You can **pray** that God will keep them calm and safe.

Children like Justin live all over our country, and they need to know that God keeps His **PROMISE** to care for them. You can help when you donate to kids in your local Foster Care system. Kids need **clothes** and **shoes** and **Christmas presents**.

To give to foster care agencies in your area or to learn how you can become a foster parent, connect with your local child welfare agency. And in some areas there are other opportunities to help foster children: becoming a mentor, guardian ad litem or CASA (court appointed advocates), or helping families who foster, by providing practical support, such as meals, transportation, babysitting, tutoring, etc.

ONEFAMILY

www.OneFamilyFL.com

Follow us on Social Media

[f] OneFamily
[o] OneFamily_fl
[▶] OneFamilyfl

www.ingramcontent.com/pod-product-compliance
Lightning Source LLC
Chambersburg PA
CBHW040022050426

42452CB00002B/91